A LifeGuide®  *Bible Study*

UDGES

Returning to God

12 studies
for individuals or groups

Donald Baker

With Notes for Leaders

IVP Connect

An imprint of InterVarsity Press
Downers Grove, Illinois

InterVarsity Press
P.O. Box 1400, Downers Grove, IL 60515-1426
World Wide Web: www.ivpress.com
E-mail: email@ivpress.com

InterVarsity Press® is the book-publishing division of InterVarsity Christian Fellowship/USA®, a student movement active on campus at hundreds of universities, colleges and schools of nursing in the United States of America, and a member movement of the International Fellowship of Evangelical Students. For information about local and regional activities, write Public Relations Dept., InterVarsity Christian Fellowship/USA, 6400 Schroeder Rd., P.O. Box 7895, Madison, WI 53707-7895, or visit the IVCF website at <www.intervarsity.org>.

Cover photograph: Greg Probst/Getty Images

ISBN 978-0-8308-3040-4

Printed in the United States of America ∞

P	21	20	19	18	17	16	15	14	13	12	11	10	9	8	7
Y	21	20	19	18	17	16	15	14	13	12	11	10	09			

Contents

GETTING THE MOST OUT OF *JUDGES* ———————————— 5

1 Judges 2:6-23   **Caught in a Cycle of Misery** ——— 9

2 Judges 3:12-30   **Breaking Free from
                            Sin's Oppression** ———————— 12

3 Judges 4   **Who Can I Trust?** ——————— 16

4 Judges 6:1-32   **Overcoming a Poor Self-Image** —— 20

5 Judges 6:33—7:22   **Changing Your Doubts to Faith** — 24

6 Judges 9   **The Importance of Character** —— 28

7 Judges 11:1-14,   **Conquering the Pain
       28—12:7   in Your Past** ———————— 32

8 Judges 13   **Preparing to Serve God** ———— 36

9 Judges 14—15   **Our Conflict with the World** ——— 40

10 Judges 16   **Accepting Your Spiritual Gifts** —— 44

11 Judges 17—18   **The Danger of False Religion** —— 47

12 Judges 19—21   **Why Morality Matters** ———— 51

LEADER'S NOTES ———————————————— 55

Getting the Most Out of *Judges*

Despicable people doing deplorable things. That pretty much sums up the book of Judges. Why would the Bible even contain such trashy tales about dysfunctional characters? As I read the book, I find it difficult to find any sympathy for those—even the heroes—involved in these violent and abusive accounts.

Who can love people who mistreat others? Who would care about people who complicate and sabotage their own lives and then refuse the hope that is offered? Who would have patience with people who refuse to learn from their mistakes but instead pass them on as a legacy to the next generation? Only God could care about creatures such as these. The book of Judges is not really about the judges who held court in Israel. It is about the God of mercy and patience who loves even the most dysfunctional and resistant among us.

The book of Judges covers the history of Israel between the death of Joshua and the appearance of Samuel (approximately 1220-1050 B.C.). For Israel this was a time without a formal government. The people were supposed to look to God for leadership, but when they failed to do so they were doomed to a continuing cycle of disobedience, suffering, cries for help and deliverance.

How can you benefit from the book of Judges? You will learn of the great depth of God's love and mercy as you see it continually offered to people who do not deserve or appreciate it. You will be able to learn from the mistakes of others. Perhaps you will be able to break cycles of dysfunction which persist in your own life or home. Most of all, the study of Judges should help you to hand the throne of your life over to God, the true King. The writer of the book of Judges often uses the phrase "in those days Israel had no king." Without God reigning in our hearts, our lives are destined to become as disastrous as the characters of this book.

To gain these benefits, it is important to study the book of Judges correctly. If you look to the characters of these stories as role models, you will be sorely disappointed. Even the judges whom God uses to save Israel are depraved and fallen creatures. The point of these stories is not the character qualities of the judges but the fact that God works through people such as these. The only true hero of this book is God.

It is also important that you refrain from becoming smug about your own enlightenment. As you read Judges, you will encounter characters who treat women as possessions and who settle problems with angry outbursts of violence (and these are supposedly the good guys!). These are stories of people in a much more primitive time who were struggling to understand God, themselves and forgiveness. Although they acted out in much more dramatic and childish ways, their passions and their rebellion against God were the same as yours and mine are. So as you read, look for the sins you have in common with the characters and ask yourself what would happen if you were to give free rein to every passion.

As you study, may you come to understand the condition of humankind and the mercy of God with new clarity and depth.

Suggestions for Individual Study

1. As you begin each study, pray that God will speak to you through his Word.

2. Read the introduction to the study and respond to the personal reflection question or exercise. This is designed to help you focus on God and on the theme of the study.

3. Each study deals with a particular passage—so that you can delve into the author's meaning in that context. Read and reread the passage to be studied. The questions are written using the language of the New International Version, so you may wish to use that version of the Bible. The New Revised Standard Version is also recommended.

4. This is an inductive Bible study, designed to help you discover for yourself what Scripture is saying. The study includes three types of questions. *Observation* questions ask about the basic facts: who, what, when, where and how. *Interpretation* questions delve into the meaning of the passage. *Application* questions help you discover the implications of the text for growing in Christ. These three keys unlock the treasures of Scripture.

Write your answers to the questions in the spaces provided or in a personal journal. Writing can bring clarity and deeper understanding of yourself and of God's Word.

5. It might be good to have a Bible dictionary handy. Use it to look up any unfamiliar words, names or places.

6. Use the prayer suggestion to guide you in thanking God for what you have learned and to pray about the applications that have come to mind.

7. You may want to go on to the suggestion under "Now or Later," or you may want to use that idea for your next study.

Suggestions for Members of a Group Study

1. Come to the study prepared. Follow the suggestions for individual study mentioned above. You will find that careful preparation will greatly enrich your time spent in group discussion.

2. Be willing to participate in the discussion. The leader of your group will not be lecturing. Instead, he or she will be encouraging the members of the group to discuss what they have learned. The leader will be asking the questions that are found in this guide.

3. Stick to the topic being discussed. Your answers should be based on the verses which are the focus of the discussion and not on outside authorities such as commentaries or speakers. These studies focus on a particular passage of Scripture. Only rarely should you refer to other portions of the Bible. This allows for everyone to participate in in-depth study on equal ground.

4. Be sensitive to the other members of the group. Listen attentively when they describe what they have learned. You may be surprised by their insights! Each question assumes a variety of answers. Many questions do not have "right" answers, particularly questions that aim at meaning or application. Instead the questions push us to explore the passage more thoroughly.

When possible, link what you say to the comments of others. Also, be affirming whenever you can. This will encourage some of the more hesitant members of the group to participate.

5. Be careful not to dominate the discussion. We are sometimes so eager to express our thoughts that we leave too little opportunity for others to respond. By all means participate! But allow others to also.

6. Expect God to teach you through the passage being discussed and through the other members of the group. Pray that you will have an enjoyable and profitable time together, but also that as a result of the study you will find ways that you can take action individually and/or as a group.

7. Remember that anything said in the group is considered confidential and should not be discussed outside the group unless specific permission is given to do so.

8. If you are the group leader, you will find additional suggestions at the back of the guide.

1

Caught in a Cycle of Misery

"Those who cannot remember the past are condemned to repeat it" (George Santayana).

GROUP DISCUSSION. If you could pass down just one lesson to your children, what would it be?

PERSONAL REFLECTION. What is the greatest lesson you have learned from your own past?

Under the inspired leadership of Joshua, the Israelite people marched into the land God had promised to give them. However, it wasn't long before the people foolishly destroyed the gift they had been given, and now they needed to be rescued. *Read Judges 2:6-23.*

1. What cycle of behavior do these verses describe?

2. What would it have been like to grow up in Israel during the last days of Joshua?

3. How did the second generation differ from the first (vv. 10-15)?

4. What do you learn from this passage about the importance of remembering and retelling the mighty acts of God?

How have you done this?

5. Describe the "great distress" (v. 15) of the Israelites.

How would ordinary citizens have been affected?

6. What lessons does God expect individuals and nations to learn from hard times?

7. What does God's work through the judges reveal about his character (vv. 16-19)?

8. Why do you think the influence of the judges was so short-lived?

9. What can you do to ensure that godly people continue to influence your life?

10. In what ways did God use and control the enemies of Israel (vv. 20-23)?

11. Verse 22 tells us the enemies "tested" Israel. What people, situations or things might God be using to test your loyalty and resolve?

The cycle of misery which trapped these Israelites is still at work today. Pray for those who are trapped in the cycle of disobedience-distress-rescue-disobedience.

Now or Later
Read Psalm 106 for a history of Israelite apostasy and rescue.

2

Breaking Free from Sin's Oppression

Judges 3:12-30

"Sins are like burrs that stick to clothes and are hard to pluck off" (Francis of Assisi).

GROUP DISCUSSION. Give each member of your group a 3 x 5 card, and ask them to complete the following sentence: "If I had never sinned, I would . . ." Read the answers and try to guess who wrote each one.

PERSONAL REFLECTION. What sins and habits do you most regret?

The Moabites were oppressing the Israelites by making them pay a heavy tax, called "tribute." Tribute was designed to keep a conquered nation so weak and in debt that they would never be able to threaten their conquerors. God sent Ehud to free his oppressed people. *Read Judges 3:12-30.*

1. What ironic twists and surprises do you find in this story?

2. How would it have felt to collect and deliver tribute to King Eglon?

_____

3. How is the oppression of Eglon similar to the oppression of sin?

_____

4. The Israelites paid a high price for ignoring God. What price have you or the people of your community paid for ignoring him?

_____

5. What plans and preparations did Ehud make in order to overthrow the evil King Eglon?

_____

6. Think of this story as an allegory in which Eglon represents the lusts and temptations you face. What does this teach you about sin?

about preparing to defeat sin?

7. Ehud's left-handedness was considered to be a handicap. Which of your weaknesses would you be surprised to find God developing into assets?

8. How is God characterized in this story?

How did he reveal himself to Ehud and the Israelites?

9. What has God promised to do for you in your fight against sin and temptation?

10. After eighteen years of subjection to the Moabites, freedom seems to have come quickly and easily. What kept the Israelites from gaining their freedom sooner?

11. Why do people today procrastinate about overcoming sin and temptation?

12. What are the "King Eglons" in your life that keep you from enjoying the freedom God promises?

What will you do about them?

Pray that God will free you from the oppression of sin and enable you to grow spiritually.

Now or Later

Read Psalm 32. What effect did sin have on the author of this psalm?

According to this psalm, how does God prevent us from being destroyed by the sins we have already committed?

What does God do to help us avoid future sin?

3

Who Can I Trust?

Judges 4

"We have to distrust each other. It's our only defense against betrayal" (Tennessee Williams).

GROUP DISCUSSION. Which of the following people do you believe to be the most trustworthy? the least trustworthy? Number the following from 1 to 10 (with 1 being the person you trust the most).

___ Myself
___ My best friend
___ College professors
___ Doctors
___ Tech support
___ Policemen
___ Pastors
___ Bankers
___ The news media
___ Lawyers

PERSONAL REFLECTION. Who or what are you trusting to get you through a crisis: spiritually, economically and physically?

The Canaanites, who next oppressed the Israelites, were powerful because they were the first culture to move from the Bronze Age to the Iron Age. They possessed nine hundred iron chariots, while the Israelites had only a few primitive weapons. How could the Israelites ever expect to overthrow such a technologically advanced enemy? *Read Judges 4.*

1. Who is your favorite character in this story: Deborah, Barak, Sisera or Jael? Why?

2. What gifts and skills did Deborah possess (vv. 4-14)?

3. How did Deborah use her skills to make a difference during a godless period of Israel's history?

4. How can you encourage the people you know to trust in God?

5. Why was it wrong for Barak to ask Deborah to go with him (vv. 8-9)?

6. In what ways should we seek others' help in obeying God's will?

7. What do we learn about Jael in verses 11 and 17-22?

8. Why do you think Jael betrayed Sisera and helped the Israelites?

9. What assumptions did Sisera make regarding his safety?

10. How did each of the things Sisera trusted for protection fail?

11. What people and things have you assumed would be there to rescue you in a crisis?

12. Compare the leading characters of this story: Deborah, Barak, Jael and Sisera. In what did each of them trust?

Which of them are you most like? Why?

13. What has this study helped you to discover about your trust in God?

Thank God that he can be trusted and ask him to show you the areas in your life where your trust may be misplaced.

Now or Later

Judges 5 retells the events of chapter 4 as a song of triumph. *Read Judges 5.* What does this chapter add to your understanding of the events in chapter 4?

God's activity is not as prominent in chapter 4 as it is in chapter 5. What did God do to rescue his people?

Since chapter 5 was written as a response to Israel's great victory, what evidence do you find that Barak came away a changed man?

4

Overcoming a
Poor Self-Image

Judges 6:1-32

"No one can make you feel inferior without your consent" (Eleanor Roosevelt).

GROUP DISCUSSION. How healthy is your self-image? Take the following quiz and compare your results with the rest of your group. (5=This is very much true of me. 1=This is not at all true of me.)

___ I have a sense of humor.
___ I am open to new ideas and experiences.
___ I project an attitude of flexibility and inventiveness.
___ I preserve harmony and dignity under stress.
___ I speak and move with ease and spontaneity.
___ I am comfortable giving and receiving compliments and affection.
___ I can speak honestly about accomplishments and shortcomings.*

PERSONAL REFLECTION. How has your self-image affected your effectiveness as a Christian?

The Midianites would make annual raids through Israel, taking what they wanted and destroying the rest. This left the Israelites feeling discouraged, weak and inferior. God had a special message for his people. *Read Judges 6:1-32.*

1. What are your first impressions of Gideon?

Would you expect him to be a hero? Why or why not?

2. Imagine life during the years of Midianite occupation (vv. 1-6). What about this situation would have been most distressing to you?

What impact would it have had on your confidence and attitude?

3. Compare the words of God to the words of Gideon in verses 7-15. How did Gideon's view of the problem and its solution differ from God's?

How did Gideon's view of himself differ from God's view of him?

4. In what ways do you feel inadequate for God's service?

5. God's words "The LORD is with you, mighty warrior" (v. 12) and "Am I not sending you?" (v. 14) can be applied to anyone God calls. For what reason is God speaking those words to you today?

6. How did the miracle in verse 21 change Gideon?

7. What events or miracles have helped you recognize God's power and presence?

8. God's first command to Gideon was to tear down his father's altar to Baal (vv. 25-27). How did Gideon's self-image get in the way of true obedience?

9. What fears have kept you from fully obeying God?

10. Gideon's cowardice almost cost him his life, but his father boldly defended him (vv. 28-32). When has God used the strengths of another person to cover your weakness?

11. Gideon was given the powerful name "Jerub-Baal" (v. 32) even though he had not really earned it. How did God help Gideon overcome his inadequacies?

12. What has this study taught you about overcoming your own inadequacies?

Pray that God will help you to overcome your inadequacies and do great things for him.

Now or Later

Read Matthew 25:14-30. What is the self-image of the one-talent servant?

How is this servant similar to Gideon?

Was the one-talent servant really inadequate? Why or why not?

What is Jesus' message in this passage to people with poor self-image?

*Adapted from *Home Health Letter* by Nathaniel Brandon in *Marriage Partnership*, March 1995.

5

Changing Your Doubts to Faith

Judges 6:33—7:22

"If a man begins with certainties, he shall end in doubts; but if he begins with doubts, he shall end in certainties" (Francis Bacon).

GROUP DISCUSSION. Hand out a slip of paper to each member of the group and ask them to write down one reason a person might have doubts about God. Then vote on which of these reasons is the most common, second most common and so on in order to develop a list of the "Top Reasons People Doubt God."

PERSONAL REFLECTION. What doubts do you have about God, and what have you done to try to answer those doubts?

Faith is shown not in how devotedly we believe but in how powerfully we take action. Though Gideon entered public life as a timid and uncertain man, constantly second-guessing himself, he did take action when God asked him to do so. Our passage for this study chronicles the metamorphosis of Gideon from reluctant leader to confident man of faith. *Read Judges 6:33—7:22.*

1. What actions did Gideon take in obedience to God?

What evidence is there that Gideon did not always feel comfortable with these steps?

2. At what point in this narrative would you have had enough proof to believe that God was going to act?

3. How did God encourage Gideon?

4. Many people have sought spiritual guidance by asking for a specific sign. Because they base this on what Gideon did in 6:36-40, this practice is sometimes referred to as "fleecing." Have you or people you know ever tried it? What happened?

5. What does Gideon's experience teach you about this practice?

What relevance do you think it has today?

6. How would Gideon have felt when over two-thirds of his men went home?

7. What kind of person was God looking for as he sifted and separated the soldiers?

Do you think that you would have qualified?

8. How would you have felt while sneaking into the Midianite camp and eavesdropping on the soldiers (7:9-12)?

9. How were Gideon and the Israelite army like a barley loaf (7:13-15)?

10. How was Gideon changed by the events in this passage?

11. What does God do today to help people who are struggling with doubt?

———————————————————————

12. Where would you place yourself on the following scale of doubt and faith? Explain.

Doubt   Faith

1   2   3   4   5   6   7   8   9   10

Pray that God will answer the doubts you are struggling with.

Now or Later

Read Matthew 14:22-33. Of all the disciples in this story, Peter seems to demonstrate the most faith, yet Jesus chastises him for having "little faith" (v. 31). Why?

What finally convinced the disciples to conclude, "Truly you are the Son of God" (v. 33)?

How is this story similar to the experience of Gideon?

to your experience?

6

The Importance of Character

"Sow an act, and you reap a habit. Sow a habit, and you reap a character. Sow a character, and you reap a destiny" (Charles Reade).

GROUP DISCUSSION. Two people are running for the same office. One has proposed political ideas that appeal to you, but you do not approve of the candidate's personal character. The other candidate has political views opposed to yours, but seems to be a person of high moral standards. Which candidate would get your vote? Why?

PERSONAL REFLECTION. What character qualities do you think are most important in a leader?

The people of Shechem followed a tyrant and refused to listen to a warning that their leader's character would bring them doom. *Read Judges 9.*

1. If you were assigned the task of writing an obituary for Abimelech, what would you say about him?

2. Which characters in this story do you sympathize with, and which don't you sympathize with? Why?

Abimelech

Jotham

Citizens of Shechem

Gaal

Zebul

Citizens of Thebez

3. When the people offered to make Gideon their king, he turned them down (8:22-23). His children apparently didn't feel the same way. What were the results of their ambitions (9:1-6)?

How did the people of Shechem get drawn into the problem?

4. In what ways does the character of your leaders affect your nation?

your church?

your Bible study group?

---

5. What truths was Jotham attempting to illustrate by his fable (vv. 7-15)?

---

6. Why do you think the people ignored Jotham's warning?

---

7. Why do we so often ignore the character flaws we find in our leaders and ourselves?

---

8. How was Jotham's prophecy (v. 20) fulfilled?

---

9. God is seldom mentioned in this chapter. What evidence can you find of his presence?

10. The story ends by stating, "Thus God repaid the wickedness" (v. 56). What does this passage teach you about God's character and justice?

_____

11. What do you as a citizen learn from this passage about the importance of choosing leaders who have a strong moral character?

about being such a person?

Pray for the character of your leaders.

Now or Later

Read 1 Timothy 3:1-12. Make a list of the character qualities that Paul tells Timothy are important for a Christian leader.

Which of these qualities are evident in your life?

How can you work to develop the character qualities that are weak?

7

Conquering the Pain in Your Past

Judges 11:1-14, 28—12:7

"Until we acknowledge painful disappointment in our circumstances and relationships, we will not pursue Christ with the passion of deep thirst" (Larry Crabb).

GROUP DISCUSSION. Draw a picture or diagram of the room in your childhood home where you spent the most time. Tell the group about the memories you associate with this place. Did you feel secure or vulnerable in this room? Accepted or rejected?

PERSONAL REFLECTION. What impact do the hurts from your past have on your life and attitudes today?

Does God love us even when our own dysfunction causes us to run from him? In the story of Jephthah, God uses a man with a broken and hurting past to illustrate what he will do to heal a broken, pain-driven world. *Read Judges 11:1-14, 28—12:7.*

---

1. Imagine that you are a psychologist, and that Jephthah and the people of Israel have come to your office for family counseling. What problems do you see in this family?

---

2. How does Jephthah's early history (11:1-3) affect his relationships with God and other people?

---

3. How have your relationships with parents and siblings affected the way you relate to God?

---

4. What expectations do Jephthah and the people of Gilead bring to their reconciliation (11:4-11)?

Are these healthy expectations? Why or why not?

5. Why does Jephthah make and keep his tragic vow to God (11:30-35)?

___

6. From Jephthah's mistake, what do you learn about making vows?

___

7. After winning a great victory and sacrificing a beloved daughter, Jephthah still has not found the approval he craves (12:1). How does Jephthah deal with this latest rejection?

___

8. How have you dealt with rejection in your life?

___

9. What advice would you give to Jephthah about finding approval?

___

10. God uses even this psychological mess to illustrate his greater salvation. What similarities do you find between Jephthah's salvation of Israel and God's salvation of us?

11. What changes would you like to make in the way you relate to other people and to God?

Pray for each member of your group as they face past hurts and seek more positive relationships.

Now or Later

Read Titus 3:3-7.What hope would verses 4-7 have offered to Jephthah?

What encouragement do these verses offer to you?

Use the wisdom of this passage to write a letter of hope to Jephthah.

8

Preparing to
Serve God

Judges 13

"Some . . . are born great, some achieve greatness, and some have greatness thrust upon them" (Shakespeare).

GROUP DISCUSSION. Imagine yourself as a tool in God's toolbox. What tool (hammer, saw, screwdriver, etc.) are you? Why?

What condition are you in?

__ Ready and waiting in the toolbox for God's next project
__ In need of sharpening, but still a good tool
__ Misplaced and can't be found
__ Currently in God's hands, working on a project
__ Being used on someone else's job site
__ Old and rusty
__ Other _____

PERSONAL REFLECTION. What steps have you taken to prepare yourself for God's service?

The birth of Samson can be compared to God's purchase of a new tool. Samson was to be set apart for God's use alone. When it was time once again to save the Israelites, God's implement of salvation would be ready at hand. *Read Judges 13.*

1. Drawing from the whole passage, how do you see this couple showing honor for God?

2. What does this suggest to you about how you could show greater honor for God?

3. What did God require of Manoah, his wife and Samson?

4. How would keeping the Nazirite vow (vv. 4-5) have prepared Samson for God's service?

5. What spiritual disciplines have you practiced?

How have you been changed by these disciplines?

6. What does God reveal about himself to Samson's parents (vv. 16-21)?

What does he hold back?

7. What additional questions would you have asked the angel if you had been Manoah?

8. Manoah received an additional revelation from God when he offered a burnt sacrifice (vv. 19-21). What have you learned about God as you have given gifts and offerings?

9. Why was Manoah afraid when he realized he had seen God (vv. 22-23)?

How did his wife reassure him?

10. Read verse 23 as if the words were being spoken directly to you. What has been God's purpose in revealing so much of himself to you?

11. What does this passage teach you about how God prepares us for service?

Pray that God will prepare each member of your group for the service he has chosen for them to do.

Now or Later

Read Luke 1:26-38. What similarities do you find between this passage and Judges 13?

How are Samson and the other judges of Israel like Jesus?

How are they different?

What does your study of Israel's judges help you to understand about the need for Jesus' birth?

about the salvation Jesus offers?

9

Our Conflict with the World

Judges 14—15

"There is in truth no such thing as harmonious coexistence between church and world, for where there is no conflict it is because the world has taken over" (Michael Wilcock).

GROUP DISCUSSION. Everyone should stand up as someone reads through the following statements. After each statement is read, those who agree with the statement move to the right side of the room, those who disagree move to the left side of the room, and those who are undecided remain in the middle.

- Our nation's government is based on Christian principles.

- It is easy to live as a Christian in today's world.

- Most business in our community is conducted according to high ethical standards.

- The poor in my city are well cared for by social agencies.

- The television and movies that I watch accurately reflect my standards.

- (For groups with singles.) The current dating practices of my peer group normally lead to positive, godly relationships.

• Minority groups are respected in my community.

• The church has a relevant message for today's culture.

PERSONAL REFLECTION. As you consider the above statements, which of them refer to issues that are important to you?

In each of the previous foreign occupations described in Judges, there is conflict. We are at least told that the people cry out to God for deliverance. Not so with the Philistine conquest—the Israelites have lived under the Philistines' thumb for forty years without complaining. In surprising ways God uses Samson to create conflict where none has existed. The message to today's church is clear: Conflict is a necessary part of our message. *Read Judges 14—15.*

1. What would it have been like to be one of Samson's companions?

2. What did Samson's parents seem to expect that their son would be like (14:1-4)?

3. How did God's plan for Samson differ from his parents' expectation?

4. When have your ideas been different from God's plan?

5. What attitude did the men of Judah have toward the Philistines (15:9-13)?

How did this attitude differ from the Israelites' feelings toward previous oppressors?

6. What is the attitude of today's Christians toward modern culture?

Is this attitude too critical, too lenient or just right? Why?

7. Samson was the only judge without an army. All of his exploits were performed single-handed. What does this tell you about the moral and spiritual condition of Israel?

8. What similarities do you see to the moral and spiritual conditions of today?

9. What did Samson's marriage and subsequent acts of vengeance accomplish?

10. In what areas should Christians be in conflict with the world?

_____

11. What are some appropriate ways in which you can express this conflict?

Ask God to help you challenge the culture around you.

Now or Later

Read Matthew 5:13-16. What are the characteristics of salt that Jesus is expecting to find in his followers?

How had Samson's countrymen lost their saltiness?

What does it mean to be a light to the world?

Why had Samson's countrymen hidden their light?

10

Accepting Your
Spiritual Gifts

Judges 16

Your spiritual gifts are the special strengths and abilities that God has given you so that you can serve him.

GROUP DISCUSSION. Have everyone write down one spiritual gift they have observed in each group member's life. Then, have the youngest member sit in the center of your group. Ask each of the other group members to tell this person what they wrote about him or her. Continue until each member has been affirmed.

PERSONAL REFLECTION. What spiritual gifts have you been given and how have you used them?

Samson represents both the best and the worst in each of us: called by the grace of God, bound to him by promise, repeatedly empowered and greatly gifted—yet faithless, self-indulgent and only too ready to fraternize with the enemy. *Read Judges 16.*

1. What do you think was Samson's tragic flaw (that is, the character defect which caused his fall)?

---

2. What was Samson's attitude toward the gifts God had given him?

---

3. What is your attitude toward the spiritual gifts God has given you?

---

4. Why do you think Samson revealed the secret of his strength to Delilah?

---

5. Why do many Christians today reject their spiritual gifts by not using them?

---

6. Imagine the scene in verse 20 when Samson discovers that the Lord has left him. What thoughts, emotions and regrets would have gone through his mind?

---

7. How would your life be different if the Lord suddenly withdrew his gifts from you?

8. How did Samson change after his capture (vv. 25-30)?

9. When Samson destroyed the temple, do you think he finally understood and accepted God's call, or was this just a last act of vengeance? Explain.

10. If Samson had accepted God's call from the very beginning, how would his life have been different?

What effect would he have had on Israel?

11. What impact can your spiritual gifts have on your church and community?

Pray that God will lead each member of your group to discover, accept and use his or her spiritual gifts.

Now or Later

There are many remarkable similarities between the life of Samson and the life of Jesus. *Read Luke 22:47—23:53.* In what way is Samson's arrest and death similar to Jesus'?

In what ways is it different?

11

The Danger of False Religion

"God created us in his image, but we have decided to return the favor and create a God who is in our image" (Tony Campolo).

GROUP DISCUSSION. Have each member of the group write a definition of a cult. After listening to each definition, discuss how you would change your answer.

PERSONAL REFLECTION. Why is it so often tempting to believe false teaching?

The last five chapters of Judges tell stories that illustrate the moral and religious degeneracy that existed during the time of the judges. The first of these stories shows how pagan worship infiltrated Israel. *Read Judges 17—18.*

1. Would you have liked living in Israel during this period of history?

Why or why not?

---

2. Describe the religion of Micah and his mother. What did they believe?

---

3. Imagine yourself in a debate with a modern-day Micah about God and religion. What would each of you say?

---

4. What was the Levite's motivation?

---

5. How did this Levite pervert religion and misrepresent God?

---

6. How have this Levite's sins continued to infect and damage the church today?

7. What do you learn about the tribe of Dan from chapter 18 (see also Joshua 19:40-48)?

8. In what ways were the people of Dan disobeying God?

9. Many people today call themselves Christians even though they disagree with some of Christ's teachings and commands. What are the results of this kind of religion?

10. The author of Judges repeats the problem several times: "In those days Israel had no king; everyone did as he saw fit." What authority has God given to keep the Christian church from straying?

11. What steps can you take to insure that your faith remains pure?

Pray that you will be well grounded in the truth of Scripture. Pray for those who have strayed from God's teachings.

Now or Later

Jesus often pointed out how the people of his day had perverted religion. For each of the passages below, answer the following questions:

• How was religion being perverted?

• What did Jesus say to correct the false teaching?

• How do Jesus' words apply to your religious practice?

Mark 7:1-23

Mark 11:12-17

Luke 11:37-52

Luke 18:9-14

12

Why Morality Matters

Judges 19—21

"If God is dead, then everything is permitted" (Friedrich Nietzsche).

GROUP DISCUSSION. Mark the following statements either true or false, then compare your answers.

___ You can't legislate morality.

___ There can be no morality apart from religion.

___ Morality depends on culture. (Cannibalism is moral in a cannibalistic culture.)

___ Morality does not change. (What was moral five hundred years ago is moral today.)

___ Christians should not get involved in politics.

PERSONAL REFLECTION. On what do you base your moral decisions?

The closing story in the book of Judges is not placed in chronological order. Rather, it is placed at the end of the book as an example of the kind of sin and rebellion God has been judging and punishing throughout the book. *Read Judges 19—21.*

---

1. What parts of this story do you find the most shocking?

---

2. Throughout these chapters, individuals are repeatedly sacrificed for dubious principles. Who is sacrificed and why?

---

3. The Levite slept while his concubine was being raped and beaten (19:25-28). How did he attempt to justify his behavior?

---

4. What role does God intend for his people to have in protecting the helpless?

---

5. How did the Israelites pervert justice in their civil war?

6. When is justice confused with vengeance in our society?

---

7. The Israelites ask God, "Why has this happened to Israel? Why should one tribe be missing from Israel today?" (21:3). How would you answer their question?

---

8. What went wrong with the Israelites' effort to reconcile with the Benjamites?

---

9. What would you have advised them to do instead?

---

10. How do you balance discipline and mercy in your relationships?

---

11. The book of Judges ends with a phrase that is repeated often, especially in the last five chapters: "In those days Israel had no king; everyone did as he saw fit." Why is the author so concerned that we know this?

12. There is a great deal of tolerance today toward people who wish to live as they see fit. What warnings does the book of Judges have for our society?

Pray for our broken and sinful society. Ask that there would be an awareness of sin and a spiritual revival.

Now or Later

Read Ephesians 4:17-24. What insights does this passage give as to why people live as they see fit?

What guidance does this passage give in making moral decisions?

How can you actually "put off your old self" (v. 22) and "put on the new self" (v. 24)?

Leader's Notes

MY GRACE IS SUFFICIENT FOR YOU. (2 COR 12:9)

Leading a Bible discussion can be an enjoyable and rewarding experience. But it can also be *scary*—especially if you've never done it before. If this is your feeling, you're in good company. When God asked Moses to lead the Israelites out of Egypt, he replied, "O Lord, please send someone else to do it!" (Ex 4:13). It was the same with Solomon, Jeremiah and Timothy, but God helped these people in spite of their weaknesses, and he will help you as well.

You don't need to be an expert on the Bible or a trained teacher to lead a Bible discussion. The idea behind these inductive studies is that the leader guides group members to discover for themselves what the Bible has to say. This method of learning will allow group members to remember much more of what is said than a lecture would.

These studies are designed to be led easily. As a matter of fact, the flow of questions through the passage from observation to interpretation to application is so natural that you may feel that the studies lead themselves. This study guide is also flexible. You can use it with a variety of groups—student, professional, neighborhood or church groups. Each study takes forty-five to sixty minutes in a group setting.

There are some important facts to know about group dynamics and encouraging discussion. The suggestions listed below should enable you to effectively and enjoyably fulfill your role as leader.

Preparing for the Study

1. Ask God to help you understand and apply the passage in your own life. Unless this happens, you will not be prepared to lead others. Pray too for the various members of the group. Ask God to open your hearts to the message of his Word and motivate you to action.

2. Read the introduction to the entire guide to get an overview of the entire book and the issues which will be explored.

3. As you begin each study, read and reread the assigned Bible passage to familiarize yourself with it.

4. This study guide is based on the New International Version of the Bible. It will help you and the group if you use this translation as the basis for your study and discussion.

5. Carefully work through each question in the study. Spend time in meditation and reflection as you consider how to respond.

6. Write your thoughts and responses in the space provided in the study guide. This will help you to express your understanding of the passage clearly.

7. It might help to have a Bible dictionary handy. Use it to look up any unfamiliar words, names or places. (For additional help on how to study a passage, see chapter five of *How to Lead a LifeGuide Bible Study*, InterVarsity Press.)

8. Consider how you can apply the Scripture to your life. Remember that the group will follow your lead in responding to the studies. They will not go any deeper than you do.

9. Once you have finished your own study of the passage, familiarize yourself with the leader's notes for the study you are leading. These are designed to help you in several ways. First, they tell you the purpose the study guide author had in mind when writing the study. Take time to think through how the study questions work together to accomplish that purpose. Second, the notes provide you with additional background information or suggestions on group dynamics for various questions. This information can be useful when people have difficulty understanding or answering a question. Third, the leader's notes can alert you to potential problems you may encounter during the study.

10. If you wish to remind yourself of anything mentioned in the leader's notes, make a note to yourself below that question in the study.

Leading the Study

1. Begin the study on time. Open with prayer, asking God to help the group to understand and apply the passage.

2. Be sure that everyone in your group has a study guide. Encourage the group to prepare beforehand for each discussion by reading the introduction to the guide and by working through the questions in the study.

3. At the beginning of your first time together, explain that these studies are meant to be discussions, not lectures. Encourage the members of the group to participate. However, do not put pressure on those who may be hesitant to speak during the first few sessions. You may want to suggest the following guidelines to your group.

☐ Stick to the topic being discussed.

☐ Your responses should be based on the verses which are the focus of the discussion and not on outside authorities such as commentaries or speakers.

☐ These studies focus on a particular passage of Scripture. Only rarely should you refer to other portions of the Bible. This allows for everyone to participate in in-depth study on equal ground.

☐ Anything said in the group is considered confidential and will not be discussed outside the group unless specific permission is given to do so.

☐ We will listen attentively to each other and provide time for each person present to talk.

☐ We will pray for each other.

4. Have a group member read the introduction at the beginning of the discussion.

5. Every session begins with a group discussion question. The question or activity is meant to be used before the passage is read. The question introduces the theme of the study and encourages group members to begin to open up. Encourage as many members as possible to participate, and be ready to get the discussion going with your own response.

This section is designed to reveal where our thoughts or feelings need to be transformed by Scripture. That is why it is especially important not to read the passage before the discussion question is asked. The passage will tend to color the honest reactions people would otherwise give because they are, of course, supposed to think the way the Bible does.

You may want to supplement the group discussion question with an icebreaker to help people to get comfortable. See the community section of *Small Group Idea Book* for more ideas.

You also might want to use the personal reflection question with your group. Either allow a time of silence for people to respond individually or discuss it together.

6. Have a group member (or members if the passage is long) read aloud the passage to be studied. Then give people several minutes to read the passage again silently so that they can take it all in.

7. Question 1 will generally be an overview question designed to briefly survey the passage. Encourage the group to look at the whole passage, but try to avoid getting sidetracked by questions or issues that will be addressed later in the study.

8. As you ask the questions, keep in mind that they are designed to be used just as they are written. You may simply read them aloud. Or you may prefer to express them in your own words.

There may be times when it is appropriate to deviate from the study guide.

For example, a question may have already been answered. If so, move on to the next question. Or someone may raise an important question not covered in the guide. Take time to discuss it, but try to keep the group from going off on tangents.

9. Avoid answering your own questions. If necessary, repeat or rephrase them until they are clearly understood. Or point out something you read in the leader's notes to clarify the context or meaning. An eager group quickly becomes passive and silent if they think the leader will do most of the talking.

10. Don't be afraid of silence. People may need time to think about the question before formulating their answers.

11. Don't be content with just one answer. Ask, "What do the rest of you think?" or "Anything else?" until several people have given answers to the question.

12. Acknowledge all contributions. Try to be affirming whenever possible. Never reject an answer. If it is clearly off-base, ask, "Which verse led you to that conclusion?" or again, "What do the rest of you think?"

13. Don't expect every answer to be addressed to you, even though this will probably happen at first. As group members become more at ease, they will begin to truly interact with each other. This is one sign of healthy discussion.

14. Don't be afraid of controversy. It can be very stimulating. If you don't resolve an issue completely, don't be frustrated. Move on and keep it in mind for later. A subsequent study may solve the problem.

15. Periodically summarize what the group has said about the passage. This helps to draw together the various ideas mentioned and gives continuity to the study. But don't preach.

16. At the end of the Bible discussion you may want to allow group members a time of quiet to work on an idea under "Now or Later." Then discuss what you experienced. Or you may want to encourage group members to work on these ideas between meetings. Give an opportunity during the session for people to talk about what they are learning.

17. Conclude your time together with conversational prayer, adapting the prayer suggestion at the end of the study to your group. Ask for God's help in following through on the commitments you've made.

18. End on time.

Many more suggestions and helps are found in *How to Lead a LifeGuide Bible Study*, which is part of the LifeGuide Bible Study series.

Components of Small Groups

A healthy small group should do more than study the Bible. There are four components to consider as you structure your time together.

Nurture. Small groups help us to grow in our knowledge and love of God. Bible study is the key to making this happen and is the foundation of your small group.

Community. Small groups are a great place to develop deep friendships with other Christians. Allow time for informal interaction before and after each study. Plan activities and games that will help you get to know each other. Spend time having fun together—going on a picnic or cooking dinner together.

Worship and prayer. Your study will be enhanced by spending time praising God together in prayer or song. Pray for each other's needs—and keep track of how God is answering prayer in your group. Ask God to help you to apply what you are learning in your study.

Outreach. Reaching out to others can be a practical way of applying what you are learning, and it will keep your group from becoming self-focused. Host a series of evangelistic discussions for your friends or neighbors. Clean up the yard of an elderly friend. Serve at a soup kitchen together, or spend a day working on a Habitat house.

Many more suggestions and helps in each of these areas are found in *Small Group Idea Book*. Information on building a small group can be found in *Small Group Leaders' Handbook* and *The Big Book on Small Groups* (both from Inter-Varsity Press). Reading through one of these books would be worth your time.

Study 1. Judges 2:6-23. Caught in a Cycle of Misery.

Purpose: To discover our tendency to drift away from God.

Question 1. An easy way to remember this cycle is by the letters *ABCD* (*Apostasy, Battering, Cry Out to God* and *Deliverance*). Another method is to remember the four R's (*Rebellion, Retribution, Repentance* and *Rescue*).

Question 2. "[Joshua's generation] was marked by two things, which belonged together: its people served the Lord, and they took possession of the land he had given them. Joshua's own burial 'within the bounds of his inheritance' (2:9) sums it up—the consummation of a long life of trusting and obeying. Not that Joshua was himself indispensable, for the same desire to find and follow the Lord's plans for them characterized his fellow-Israelites even in 'the days of the elders who outlived Joshua'; the crucial factor was that there were still in Israel a personal knowledge of the Lord's redeeming work, and people who had directly experienced the rescue from Egypt and the molding of a new nation" (Michael Wilcock, *The Message of Judges* [Downers Grove, Ill.: InterVarsity Press, 1992], p. 28).

Question 3. "[The second generation] 'did not know the Lord or the work which he had done for Israel'. Consequently, in the words which will become all too familiar, 'the people of Israel did what was evil in the sight of the Lord.' The evil is simple, but profound, and it has its equivalent in every age. Exchanging the God of classical, historical redemption for the nature gods who dominate the thinking of most ordinary people around you (2:12)—what could be more sensible? For the nature gods, of course, wear a variety of disguises. In the days of the judges they were called Dagon and Baal; nowadays they are anything from New Age pantheism to the market forces of economics. All of them are powers which are excitingly bigger than you, but which you can nevertheless manipulate to your own ends" (Wilcock, *Message of Judges*, p. 28).

Question 4. "When Joshua's generation died out, the next generation lacked that personal knowledge of God which is the heart of biblical faith and quickly forgot all that he had done for their nation. This is a 'generation gap' of the most profound and challenging kind, and, as usual, both sides were to blame . . . . Somehow the Joshua generation, though they had personally experienced so much of God's goodness, failed to keep the record of his mighty acts alive. If we do not tell what God has done and keep the memory fresh and vibrant, the past will die and its lessons with it" (David Jackman, *Judges, Ruth,* Mastering the Old Testament, vol. 7 [Dallas: Word, 1991], p. 53).

Question 5. "Israel was harried, enslaved and enfeebled, and, through the operation of the law of cause and effect (the sapping of its spiritual strength by the sensuous Baal cult being accompanied by a corresponding decline in its moral and physical vitality), the nation was brought into deep distress. Their forsaking of the Lord had one further consequence. Since the bond which united the nation was primarily a religious one, centered in the covenant and expressed in worship at the amphictyonic shrine, the weakening of the bond led to a weakening of their unity and they became disorganized and divided" (Arthur E. Cundall, *Judges and Ruth,* Tyndale Old Testament Commentaries, vol. 7 [Downers Grove, Ill.: InterVarsity Press, 1968], p. 69).

Question 7. God's work through the judges reveals his anger against sin, his patience with our disobedience and his forgiveness of people who do not deserve it.

Question 8. "How could a people who had seen so much of the power of God drift so far from him? It did not happen all at once. It never does.

1. *They lost fellowship with God by incomplete obedience.* When Israel did not drive out the people as God commanded, they were sowing the seeds of their own spiritual failure.

2. *They did not consciously remind themselves of the grace of God.* They for-

sook God, when they forgot all that He had done for them.

3. *They rejected the Word of God.* Israel began to look at life the way the Canaanites did. Instead of being controlled by the truths of Scripture, they were controlled by the opinions and impulses of their sinful natures" (Gary Inrig, *Hearts of Iron, Feet of Clay* [Chicago: Moody Press, 1979], p. 38).

Question 10. The other nations living in Canaan thought that they were exercising their independence and surviving on their own power. Little did they realize that God was allowing their evil behavior only to test the obedience of his own people.

Study 2. Judges 3:12-30. Breaking Free from Sin's Oppression.

Purpose: To find freedom from the sins and temptations that threaten our spiritual growth.

Question 1. "In their security, the Moabites made a series of assumptions which were all belied in the event. The king of Moab assumed his visitor was unarmed and handicapped, but it was not so. His courtiers assumed they ought to leave his door locked, but it was not so. His troops assumed no Israelites would dare attack them, but it was not so" (Wilcock, *Message of Judges,* p. 44).

Question 2. The demand for tribute was commonly used to weaken an enemy. By forcing a country to pay tribute, the conqueror was able to impoverish the weaker state while increasing its own revenues. Tribute also served as a simple instrument of administration. If a subjected country failed to send its annual tribute, this would be taken as a sign of rebellion, and a military regiment would be sent to deal with the insurrection.

Question 3. Having to pay tribute was a constant reminder that your nation had been defeated. It kept people chained to their past, always paying for what had happened long ago and unable to change or move forward to a better life.

Question 5. King Eglon certainly would not have let just anyone deliver the tribute, nor would he have consented to a private meeting with someone he did not trust. Ehud had carefully planned the elements of deception: the guise of an envoy, the left hand, the hidden sword, the pretended message and the locked door

Question 6. If Eglon represents the lusts and temptations you face, then the tribute represents the consequences of those sins, the Israelites' cry to God is our cry for forgiveness, and Ehud's double-edged sword is the power of God's Word and the Holy Spirit (our secret weapons against temptation). Michael Wilcock writes: "In 3:29, . . . the Moabite soldiers are described as *shamen,* 'stout'. The Hebrew word, like the English one, can be taken in two ways: as long as you fear them, they seem 'strong', and indeed they are 'all . . . able-bodied'; but once they are leaderless, they are (metaphorically) merely 'fat'—the fearsome muscle is seen to be nothing but flesh" (Wilcock, *Message of Judges,* pp. 44-45).

Question 7. The term *left-handed* is used here in the same way that you would call a person "near-sighted." The emphasis is that Ehud did not have use of his right hand. Perhaps it was even deformed or paralyzed in some way. Ironically, Ehud belonged to the tribe of Benjamin, a name which means "son of the right hand." Michael Wilcock comments, "We are not to be surprised if [God] chooses the most unlikely methods, even if we find that such 'left-handed' things as deprivation or illness, frustration or failure, become the instruments of his rule. After all, who would have expected that he would choose to work through such a 'left-handed' crowd of people as the Christian church? Who would have predicted that when the Judge came himself in the flesh, he would come as such a 'left-handed' person, with 'no form or comeliness that we should look at him, and no beauty that we should desire him . . . despised and rejected by men (Is. 51:2-3)?' " (Wilcock, *Message of Judges,* pp. 46-47).

Question 8. "It was God who raised up Ehud, and, as verse 28 shows, Ehud was very conscious that the battle was the Lord's. 'The Lord has given your enemies the Moabites into your hands.' Ehud recognized . . . that it was not his cleverness or his competence which produced the victory, but the power of God" (Inrig, *Hearts of Iron, Feet of Clay,* pp. 51-52).

Question 9. God demonstrates over and over again that he is eager to forgive, renew, restore and retrain us for his service.

Question 10. For eighteen years the Israelites had failed to call out to God, repent or admit they had a problem that they could not solve on their own. During this time they continued to pay tribute to Moab, hoping that this would bring them peace. They had settled for this existence as a conquered country, not understanding or believing that God had something much better in mind for them.

Study 3. Judges 4. Who Can I Trust?

Purpose: To demonstrate that trust in God is well-placed, while trust in anything else will fail.

Question 2. Deborah demonstrates many gifts: wisdom in deciding disputes, administration in delegating responsibility, prophecy in telling Barak what will happen and courage in leading people into battle. Since the people of Deborah's day would not normally have accepted a woman in such a leadership role, she must have also been blessed with a great deal of confidence, boldness and vision.

Question 3. "Deborah was not a more brilliant tactician than had been seen for a couple of decades in Israel; she was a channel of divine revelation, the leader specially raised up by God for this time. As with every true spiritual gift, this was recognized, not because she wore a badge, or carried a diploma or even announced herself as possessing it, but just because people were so consistently and regularly helped by her ministry. That is the biblical way a gift has to be tested and proved" (Jackman, *Judges, Ruth,* p. 83).

Question 5. "The real flaw in Barak's character is shown in the fact that having received God's call through Deborah, he tried to make his obedience conditional (4:8). Whenever we start to bargain with God about the clear terms of his Word which demand our obedience, we are bound to be wrong-footed. 'If . . . then, . . . but if not, then I will not . . .' is a formula which is always an affront to God in his dealings with us. There can be no 'if' in a response of obedient faith. In fact, Barak seems to have more confidence in the presence of Deborah than in the Word of the Lord, so it is not surprising that his lack of real trust precludes him from sharing the glory of the victory" (Jackman, *Judges, Ruth,* p. 85).

Question 6. It is not wrong to seek help in obeying God's will. God normally wants us to work together, seeking advice where needed and delegating responsibilities. Barak was not wrong in asking for Deborah's help. What was wrong was that he seemed to find his strength and courage in her rather than in God.

Question 8. Jael's husband, Heber, was friendly with both sides in this conflict, yet Jael secretly sympathized with Israel and the religion of Israel. It is doubtful, however, that Jael felt called to render God's justice against Sisera. It is more likely that she did not want Barak to find Sisera in her tent. By killing him, she saw an opportunity to cement a friendship with the conqueror.

Question 9. Sisera assumed that his nine hundred chariots would be able to defeat the Israelites easily, that his friendship with Heber (v. 17) would mean that Heber and his wife, Jael, would give him refuge, and that no one would expect to find him in a woman's tent.

Question 10. According to Judges 5:4, 20-21, Sisera's chariots probably became stuck in the mud during a well-timed thunderstorm and the resulting flood.

Question 12. Deborah trusted God; Barak trusted a godly person; Jael trusted herself; Sisera trusted in his superior weapons' technology.

Study 4. Judges 6:1-32. Overcoming a Poor Self-Image.

Purpose: To learn to take our eyes off our own inadequacies and trust God's power through us.

Question 2. The Midianites were nomads who made annual raids through

Israel's territory. Unable to stop these raids, the Israelites were forced to leave their homes and cities and live primitively in caves to hide from their oppressors. By using camels, the Midianites were able to create a speedy and long-range fighting force.

Question 3. "The complaint of Gideon was doubtless shared by most of his contemporaries: the Lord had forsaken them; his mighty exploits were in the past, not the present. Nor was Gideon convinced by the assurance in the Lord's reply (v. 14) that deliverance was at hand. Instead he described himself as the least likely person for such an assignment. The words may indicate his natural humility, but may also be based on the hard facts of experience. Gideon knew just how poor his father was at this time of crisis" (Cundall, *Judges and Ruth*, p. 105).

Question 5. "In many ways, Gideon embodies within himself and his situation the fate of the whole nation—defeatist and negative without hope or vision, under Midian's heel. But God sees the man that he will make and it is on that basis that he greets Gideon. It seems to be all wrong. The 'mighty man of valor' is timid and inexperienced, is hiding from the enemy and working for his father Joash, who is actually a priest of a pagan shrine. Again, the Bible is stressing the ingenuity and sublime resourcefulness of God. He loves to take the most unlikely clay to mold his choice vessels" (Jackman, *Judges, Ruth*, p. 107).

Question 6. The fire flaring from the rock and consuming the meat convinced Gideon that his offering had been accepted and he was in the presence of God. This experience changed him from a defeated man hiding out in a winepress to a leader who began to initiate action against the enemy.

Question 8. If Gideon had been more confident, he would have taken a more public stand against idolatry. By destroying the altar during the night, Gideon obeyed everything God told him to do, but avoided speaking out as a prophet.

Questions 10. "When Joash realized what God had done, I believe that he was both shamed and challenged. He knew that Gideon's actions were right, and that he should have done the same thing years earlier. So he defended Gideon in a striking way. 'Listen, what you are doing is blasphemy. If Baal really is God, he does not need you to defend him. If he cannot defend himself, he is not worthy of worship. If he is really God, Gideon will be struck dead.' It was a basic lesson in Baal theology! Gideon had been so fearful of his father and his family that he had attacked the altar in the darkness of night. Now the man that he most feared had become his greatest defender. How often that is true. Our obedience to the Lord Jesus can do great things in the lives of the most unexpected people. People whose reactions we fear the most are often the first to respond when they see the reality of our commitment to Christ" (Inrig, *Hearts of Iron, Feet of Clay*, p. 103).

Question 11. "Jerub-Baal" literally means "let Baal contend," but for Gideon it came to mean "Baal conqueror." God was the one who made Gideon into a Baal conqueror by calling him, giving him repeated assurances that he could become a leader, and then telling him exactly what to do.

Study 5. Judges 6:33—7:22. Changing Your Doubts to Faith.

Purpose: To demonstrate that faith increases as we obey God's directives.

Question 1. Gideon obeyed God first by summoning the people to battle and then by sending most of his volunteers home. Even though he obeyed, he seemed to question what he had done. For example, after sending out the call for a volunteer army, Gideon asked for a sign that God would really carry through with his plan. After all but three hundred men were sent home, God again helped Gideon overcome his fear.

Question 3. God gave Gideon much special encouragement. First, he used Gideon's summons to bring together an army of 32,000 volunteers. Next, God twice confirmed Gideon's calling with the miracles of the fleece. Finally, God gave Gideon even more encouragement by allowing him to eavesdrop on enemies discussing a dream. "Here the Lord is coaxing along a reluctant leader who really is 'diffident, modest and shy,' and who needs to have his confidence built up step by step by a patient, loving, but determined God" (Wilcock, *Message of Judges*, p. 82).

Question 5. It is important to notice that Gideon knew what God wanted him to do even before he put out the fleece. In fact, Gideon had sent out the call for an army before he asked God for this sign. Gideon asked God for a sign not to discover God's will but to be reassured in spite of self-doubt. It is also enlightening to recognize that the first miracle of the fleece was not enough to give Gideon confidence. Even the second miracle didn't seem to fully convince Gideon, and so God gave the Midianite dream (7:9-14) as a third confirmation. Although God may be gracious to confirm our calling by spectacular means, the only way that any of us can be fully convinced of God's will is to take action and do what God has said.

Question 6. The precedent for sending the fearful soldiers home comes from Deuteronomy 20:8. God commanded that before a battle the officers were to release those who were fainthearted so that they would not discourage the rest of the soldiers.

Question 7. Scholars are not sure of the significance of the drinking test.

Some think that those who lapped with their hands showed greater alertness. Others believe that there was no significance to the way they drank. God merely used this as a sign to show Gideon which men he wanted. He could just as well have picked all men wearing a blue shirt or all those who were blond. All of God's actions were signs to Gideon that the battle was won by the power of God and not the power of Gideon's army.

Question 8. "God knew exactly what Gideon's problem was. He was still afraid! We need to remember that the problems we face which we are unwilling to confess and lay out before God are equally transparently obvious to him. After the episodes with the fleece, Gideon may well have felt that he dare not ask God for anything more. The lovely touch in this passage is that God takes the initiative and comes to speak to Gideon. He meets the man of faith as his knees are knocking in order to minister his grace and encouragement to him" (Jackman, *Judges, Ruth*, p. 128).

Question 9. Barley was thought to be an inferior grain, worth only half as much as wheat. Although it seems impossible that a loaf of bread (and one of only half value at that) could knock over a tent, that is what God does. Only God could cause a stale old loaf of bread (like the Israelite nation) to overcome the Midianite army.

Question 10. Gideon came to understand "that it was not a battle between 300 Israelites and 135,000 Midianites. It was God who was fighting Midian, and the 300 men were just his channels. Right there, beside a Midianite camp, Gideon learned the greatest lesson of his life, and he bowed in worship before God. For the first time, Gideon had come to realize the greatness of God. In a very real sense we are never prepared for battle until we know what it is to bow in worship before God. . . . Notice what Gideon said as he went back to his little band of men, 'Arise, for the Lord has given the camp of Midian into your hands' (v. 15). Gideon had become strong because God had taught him that victory is not gained by self-confidence but by God-confidence" (Inrig, *Hearts of Iron, Feet of Clay*, p. 130).

Study 6. Judges 9. The Importance of Character.

Purpose: To demonstrate the need to be a person of high moral character and to choose leaders who exhibit such character.

Question 1. Abimelech was the illegitimate son of Gideon. With the aid of his mother's family, he killed all of his seventy brothers (except Jotham, the youngest, who escaped). He had himself declared king. A revolt, led by Gaal, was cruelly suppressed. However, while taking vengeance on his enemies, Abimelech was killed by a woman who dropped a millstone on his head in self-defense. Adjectives that might describe Abimelech are *angry, vengeful, despotic, murderous* and *ambitious.*

Question 3. "Abimelech persuaded his Shechemite relatives that his Israelite half-brothers would seize control unless they were eliminated, and he were made king instead. The leaders of Shechem agreed. The massacre of Abimelech's rivals was financed by funds from the temple of Baal-Berith, and his coronation duly took place 'by the oak of the pillar at Shechem.' . . . The story of Abimelech is set at the heart of the book of Judges to show what happens when obligations are not kept, when truth and integrity are rejected. There is no longer any [leader of strong character] to bring the weight of his authority to bear, but that places all the greater responsibility on an Israel who does in fact know very well how she should be serving the Lord" (Wilcock, *Message of Judges,* pp. 93-94).

Question 5. "Like Israel, the trees are looking for a king, but no one wants the job. The olive, fig, and vine all decline for the same basic reason. They will not tear themselves from the soil, in which they have been planted and bear their fruit, in order 'to sway over trees.' The verb literally means to float about or soar above. Oil, figs, and wine are among the most valuable products of the land of Israel. The trees' argument, therefore, is that they are not willing to leave the useful tasks they are currently performing in order to take on the dubious privilege of an exalted, but uncertain, superiority, waving over the other trees. The concept behind it makes its own comment on the value, or otherwise, of the kingly office. However, rather than reject the idea of having a king at all, the desperate trees approach the totally unsuitable bramble, or thornbush. But because all the trees are now involved (v. 14), it seems that no other candidate is forthcoming. The bramble is only too pleased to accept. After all, it has no useful task to perform, and nothing to offer but thorns. The shelter of its shade is insufficient to protect anyone from the burning sun. It has nothing positive to give, for the trees will soon discover that all it can do is to hurt and wound" (Jackman, *Judges, Ruth,* pp. 158-59).

Question 6. "We need to remind ourselves at this point of the basic lesson of Judges 9. If God is not King, an usurper will arise in his place. If God had been kept in his place as King, Abimelech would never have been successful. But when there is a spiritual vacuum, Satan will rush in to fill it" (Inrig, *Hearts of Iron, Feet of Clay,* p. 163).

Question 8. Arthur Cundall describes it well when he states, "Self-seeking opportunists and those capable of treacherous murder never make easy companions, and it was not long before a breach occurred between Abimelech and the men of Shechem" (*Judges and Ruth,* p. 130). The Shechemites started the trouble when they set armed bands in ambush along the trade routes (v. 25). This action deprived Abimelech of the dues which he normally would have collected from passing caravans. It also made Abimelech look bad, since he could not guarantee safe travel in his own domain.

Question 9. Be sure to note God's sovereign action in verse 23. The prophecy of Jotham was made in God's power and then carried out by him.

Question 10. This text reminds us that God is in control. "Yes, he does permit the evil to thrive and develop, with disastrous consequences, but he also limits its extent. He cuts Abimelech short in the midst of his career. He extinguishes the flames when they seem certain to spread and overwhelm the whole land. . . . The whole perspective is changed when we begin to understand this sad chapter as a record of covenant discipline, expressing the loving faithfulness of our God. He cares what his people do with their lives and whom they worship. He will stop at nothing to win them back to that personal relationship of trust and love for which he redeemed them" (Jackman, *Judges, Ruth,* p. 166).

Study 7. Judges 11:1-14, 28—12:7. Conquering the Pain in Your Past.

Purpose: To discover and correct dysfunctional ways in which we relate to God and one another.

Question 2. After being rejected by his brothers, Jephthah's desire for acceptance seemed to color all of his relationships. Judges 11:3 tells us that he gathered a group of outlaws who would accept him. When Jephthah's brothers asked for help, his primary concern was "Will I really be your head?" He tried to buy God's acceptance with a sacrifice (11:31). When his leadership was criticized, he responded by waging war on the critics (12:1-6).

Question 4. The elders of Gilead, who had never found Jephthah useful before, now hoped that they could take advantage of his strength and fighting ability. Jephthah, who had never been wanted before, hoped that people would now accept and admire him.

Question 5. God had made it clear in the law of Moses that human sacrifice was a detestable thing (Lev 18:21; 20:2-5; Deut 12:31; 18:10). Why then did Jephthah make such a rash vow? He was so anxious to perform well in battle that he was willing to pay any price for success. Arthur Cundall comments, "It is certain that this was intended as an act of devotion on Jephthah's part, a recompense for God's action through him; but had he been better versed in the traditions of Moses he would have known that God does not desire to be honored in this way. The 'fruit of my body' (or anyone else's body) cannot be offered 'for the sin of my soul,' or as a mark of devotion to the Lord (Micah

6:6-8). The lives of others are sacred and are not to be terminated for the private end of an individual, however laudable that end may appear. As Bishop Hall observed, 'It was his zeale to vow, it was his sin to vow rashly' " (*Judges and Ruth,* pp. 146-47).

Question 6. "Jephthah's action is showing us something that is endemic in the human heart. We all tend to act this way. We Christians say we believe in God's unconditional love, but when we get into a tight scrape our lives betray us. We begin to bargain with God, because we don't really trust him. We so desperately want to see his power at work on our behalf, to improve our circumstances, or grant us what we call success, that we offer him anything if he will only intervene. And that is really creating God in *our* image, in our human faithlessness, rather than believing his revelation, as, for example, it is declared in the ringing assurances of Romans 8:31-39. The tragedy is that Jephthah had no need to make the vow. God was already with him. The Spirit of the Lord was already upon him. But Jephthah's experience of the Spirit, in common with all the great heroes of the Old Testament, lacked the personal dimension of indwelling, which is the birthright of the New Testament believer" (Jackman, *Judges, Ruth,* p. 198).

Question 7. Rather than being hailed as a hero as he expected, Jephthah was criticized by the Ephraimites, who complained that they had been slighted by not being called to the battle. In earlier years, when Jephthah had been rejected by his brothers he ran away. This time he lashed out in angry vengeance.

Question 9. "Some of us have had a raw deal out of life, but we need to recognize that God's providence means that he weaves the strands together to make each of us the unique individual we all are, and that is for his glory. There are no mistakes, no accidents with God: no pages to be torn up. It all counts. The story of Jephthah provides us with a key example to encourage our 'no hopers' not to write themselves out of the script, but to make themselves freshly available to their totally ingenious Lord" (Jackman, *Judges, Ruth,* p. 186).

Question 10. This question presumes that the members of your group are familiar with the gospel of Jesus Christ. If they are not, use this opportunity to show that Jephthah paralleled Christ in several ways. Both were "despised and rejected by men" (Is 53:3). Jephthah sacrificed his only daughter as God sacrificed his only son. The daughter went into the hills and wept, but she was a willing sacrifice, just as Jesus wept and prayed in the garden but went willingly to the cross.

Study 8. Judges 13. Preparing to Serve God.

Purpose: To help group members identify God's work in their lives to prepare them for service.

Background. After repeated periods of apostasy, numerous rescues and eleven judges, now the people of Israel don't even bother to repent anymore. For forty years Israel has been in the hands of the Philistines, but the people don't seem to notice that anything is wrong. This time there is no cry for deliverance. Still, God does not abandon his people. He makes a personal visit to a faithful couple to promise a savior named Samson.

Question 1. Both Manoah and his wife believed the angel's message. They had no doubt that they were to become parents and that their son was to be raised in a special way. Manoah prayed that the "man of God" would return not because he doubted the message but because he wanted to make sure he understood the instructions. Clearly, Manoah intended to obey whatever instructions he was given. Manoah's wife showed great confidence in God's words when she told her husband that since God had made a promise, they would certainly have to live long enough for it to happen (v. 23).

Question 3. "The Nazirite vow is delineated in Numbers 6:1-21 and contains three stipulations: the Nazirite was to abstain from all products of the vine; his hair was to be left uncut during the period of his vow; he was not to defile himself by contact with a dead body. In view of the unique character of the son she was to bear, Manoah's wife was to share the requirements of a Nazirite by abstaining from wine (made from grapes), strong drink (made from fruit, honey and grain), and unclean food (which may be a direct reference to Numbers 6:3-4, or a more general injunction to pay particular attention to the Israelite dietary laws)" (Cundall, *Judges and Ruth,* pp. 156-57).

Question 4. "The great danger posed by the Philistines was assimilation, and in contrast to that, Samson was a living embodiment of separation, a lifelong Nazirite under the vow of God. True, he was a man separated from certain things, but most of all, he was a man separated unto the Lord. It is right there that the tragedy of Samson lies, because Samson's separation turned out to be purely negative. He vowed not to take wine, not to cut his hair, and not to go near the dead. He knew the code, but he did not understand the concept. The point of the Nazirite vow was not separation from, it was separation unto. If it was not in the code, Samson went ahead and did it, but he lacked a warm-hearted love for God. By his position, Samson was dedicated to the will of God. But in his heart, he was not dedicated to the God whose will it was. His separation was formal and legalistic" (Inrig, *Hearts of Iron, Feet of Clay,* pp. 213-14).

Question 6. Manoah was asking more than might appear to us when he petitioned the Lord to tell his name. For the people of this time, a name was more than just an identification. It also suggested the person's character. The Lord's name was so holy that no one even dared to pronounce it.

Question 8. "Thankfulness is perhaps the way in which we express our faith most clearly. . . . It is all too easy to occupy our time with what we fondly imagine are more productive, or at least more necessary, activities. We are concerned about time to eat, time to talk—these are part of our humanity and must not be denied. But as with any other part of life, we can overemphasize the trivial and spend too much time on a self-centered activism, which subtly pushes life out of its true perspective. Heaven is concerned about time to thank, time to worship, time to reflect on the nature of God, to rejoice in his goodness and enjoy his friendship" (Jackman, *Judges, Ruth,* p. 214).

Question 9. To see God's face was believed to bring death (Gen 32:30; Ex 33:20). There are limitations to human comprehension of God. Manoah was afraid that he might now know too much. His wife, however, knew that once God has spoken, he will not go back on his word. Since God had promised them a son, she had every confidence they would live to raise a son.

Question 11. Samson's life shows us what strength God gives to those who are dedicated to him: "It was to be a living demonstration to Israel (and to the church) that God's strength can transcend human weakness, when that weakness is consecrated to him. Our problem is that we do not really believe that to be true. We imagine that we have to find resources of strength or capability within ourselves and, consequently, we tend to spend inordinate amounts of energy and effort on trying to generate within ourselves that which God has already promised to give us" (Jackman, *Judges, Ruth,* pp. 216-17).

Study 9. Judges 14—15. Our Conflict with the World.

Purpose: To understand that living for God means conflict with the world.

Question 2. The angel had told Samson's mother that her son would "begin the deliverance of Israel from the hands of the Philistines" (13:5). It must have been quite a disappointment when Samson came home and announced that he wished to marry a Philistine instead of fighting them. Because Samson had been raised as a Nazirite dedicated to God, his parents would also have expected their son to spark a return to the Lord as leaders like Gideon had done.

Question 3. "The author explicitly states that the Spirit of the Lord drove him to do all this. The Spirit seized him and filled him with power so that he could punish the Philistines. . . . He was acting as a judge called by God who wanted to demonstrate to the Philistines that he was their most formidable foe. It was really the Lord, Israel's covenant God, who was fighting through

Samson against the oppressor of his people" (C. J. Goslinga, *Joshua, Judges and Ruth,* trans. Ray Togtman, The Bible Students' Commentary [Grand Rapids, Mich.: Zondervan, 1968], p. 428).

Question 4. We limit God when we expect him to act just as we would—through the people we like best or the denominations we have chosen.

Question 5. When the men of Judah ask, "Why have you come to fight us?" (15:10), they show that they are completely mystified as to why there should be any conflict with the Philistines. In the past, living under foreign powers had caused the Israelites to long for God. They would cry out in anguish for release so that they could again bind themselves to God. This time, the people seem to have found life under the Philistines acceptable.

Question 7. Samson didn't receive help from his people because the people had fallen away from God and accepted the ways of the Philistines. The Israelites found that they could have peace with this enemy as long as they didn't make waves.

Question 8. We live in a world that fears conflict. Tolerance dictates that we accept all beliefs as equally valid. Therefore, we have become silent about right and wrong, truth and error.

Question 9. "The key must be in 14:4. 'The Lord . . . was seeking an occasion against the Philistines.' Samson's fraternizing with the enemy expresses in one individual what the attitude of the nation at large had become. But the tribes of Canaan still *were* enemies of Israel, and Israel's distinctiveness was meant to be seen in confrontation and contrast with them. By the time of Samson, Israel has so accommodated herself to the world around her that . . . she wants no rocking of the boat. Like Samson, she is willing, even eager, to marry into Philistine society. The force of 14:4 is that the two communities are so interlocked that even the Lord can find nothing to get hold of to push them apart. He uses Samson's weakness, therefore, to bring about the relationship with this irresistible girl from which so much ill-feeling will flow, and in the process he gives Samson his supernatural strength and the first opportunities to use it. With the lion the young man discovers his gift, and with the slaughter at Ashkelon he finds its purpose" (Wilcock, *Message of Judges,* p. 139).

Study 10. Judges 16. Accepting Your Spiritual Gifts.

Purpose: To encourage group members to discover, accept and use their spiritual gifts.

Question 1. There are several flaws that contributed to Samson's downfall: his insistence on having whatever he desired, his pride and his desire to

please. Also contributing was Samson's assumption that he could accept
God's gifts without accepting God's call. He thought that his strength was
given for his own personal use and could never be taken from him. Not until
God left him (v. 20) did Samson seem to realize that God had been with him.
It never occurred to him until perhaps the very last act of his life that God
had gifted him for a purpose beyond himself.

Question 2. Samson was living for himself. He appreciated God's gifts
because they enabled him to get what he wanted, but he had no interest in
using his gifts for God's intended purpose. He went to Gaza for a night of sex-
ual pleasure. He then carried off the gates of the city—not because God had
called him to do so, but as a prank to embarrass his enemies. Although Samson continued to follow God's plan in driving a wedge between the Israelites
and the Philistines, he did not seem to have any awareness of God's presence
in his life.

Question 4. Samson had already broken other parts of his Nazirite vow with
no ill effects. Perhaps he believed that God could not or would not take away
his strength. Samson may also have tired of being a one-man army. He did not
value his strength and may have thought that without it he could live as a
normal person.

Question 5. Some reasons Christians do not use their spiritual gifts are that
they want to serve themselves rather than God, they feel inadequate, and they
would prefer to have some other gift.

Question 8. "Samson's defeat at the hands of the Philistines, permitted by
God, was the first time in his life that he hit a brick wall he could not break
his way through. He lost his sight and he lost his strength. He realized the
unchanging reality of his own weakness. . . . Only when our foolishness fails
do we begin to see what our hearts are really like. It took his failure and
abject humiliation to show Samson that he was not a strong man after all—
only a weak man in whom God had demonstrated his mighty power. When
we learn that, weak people like us become usable. Like Samson, we learn to
depend upon God in a new, even desperate, way, which is the essence of true
faith" (Jackman, *Judges, Ruth*, p. 257).

Question 9. "Ironically it is in a hostile place of foreign worship that Samson
utters his first *formal* prayer to God (contrast 15:18). Equally it is only after
he has been brought low that he needs to ask for help. He had not himself
asked for the gift of great strength. It had been granted to him, and the
accompanying Nazirite vow had been laid upon his mother, not himself. . . .
God's spirit had always come to him unasked when necessary. But now, hum-
bled and blinded, the butt of cruel sport like many a later victim in the arena,

he knew he was in need. We do not require to know we are in need for God to come to our aid. But we do need to know that, whenever and wherever we are in need, we may ask for help. That brings its own death-defying dignity to Samson 'eyeless in Gaza' " (A. Graeme Auld, *Joshua, Judges, and Ruth* [Philadelphia: Westminster Press, 1984], p. 221).

Question 10. "Samson had spiritual power and performed feats which an ordinary man would hardly perform. But he was unconscious of his high vocation. . . . He did not realize that physical endowments no less than spiritual are gifts from God, and that to retain them we must be obedient. . . . Samson was a wild, self-willed man. Passion ruled. He could not resist the blandishments of women. In short, he was an overgrown schoolboy, without self-mastery. He accordingly wrought no permanent deliverance for Israel; he lacked the spirit of cooperation. He undertook a task far too great for even a giant single-handed. Yet, it must be allowed that Samson paved the way for Saul and David. He began the deliverance of Israel from the Philistines. He must, therefore, be judged according to his times. In his days there was unrestrained individual independence on every side, each one doing as he pleased. Samson differed from his contemporaries in that he was a hero of faith (Heb 11:32). He was a Nazirite and therefore dedicated to God. He was given to revenge, yet he was ready to sacrifice himself in order that his own and his people's enemies might be overthrown. He was willing to lay down his own life for the sake of his fellow tribesmen—not to save his enemies, however, but to kill them" (George L. Robinson, "Samson" in *The International Standard Bible Encyclopaedia* [Grand Rapids, Mich.: Eerdmans, 1939], pp. 2676-77).

Study 11. Judges 17—18. The Danger of False Religion.

Purpose: To show that distorted images of God and religion lead to moral and spiritual chaos.

Question 2. Micah's mother believed that she was able to manipulate God into bringing blesses and curses on people. She thought that she could please God by making grand promises, even though she did not keep them (notice that although she consecrated all 1,100 shekels of silver, she only gave 200). Micah believed that he could worship God through molten and carved images, set up a shrine in his home and establish his own priesthood—all in direct contradiction of God's commands. Micah's religion is best expressed in 17:13: "Now I know that the LORD will be good to me, since this Levite has become my priest." He wanted to avoid trouble and have God bless him with a life of wealth, comfort and ease.

Question 3. "The essence of idolatry is to want to bring God within our pockets, so as to control him. Foolishly, we imagine that we can deal with the source of life on the same level as ourselves, so that we can bribe him, or drive a bargain, or compel him to do what we want, to give us what we want out of life. Above all, and at all costs, what natural human beings want is a god that will not make demands on our lives—one that will give us what we need, but require nothing in return. It may be an attractive shape or a quality product; it can be a status symbol much admired and envied. But we worship idols for their imagined power, which is given into our hands as their devotees. In that sense, all forms of idolatry are an extension of works-oriented religion, a man-made invention by which I hope to save myself by the works of my own hands" (Jackman, *Judges, Ruth*, p. 263).

Question 4. The Levites were made priests by God, who had made special provisions concerning where they were to live and how they were to be supported (Num 18:8-24). This priest was an opportunist who was willing to sell his services to the highest bidder.

Question 5. In order to obtain and keep his job, the Levite had to support the beliefs of his benefactor. He allowed Micah to believe that he would be blessed through the presence of a Levite priest. He set up a place of worship where it was not allowed (Deut 12:4-14), and he included the idol that Micah had made.

Question 6. "Listen to a church council or a congregational meeting discussing the sort of minister the church wants to call. So often, what God wants is assumed to be the same as what we want, because in practice God has become a pocket-sized idol. What churches always need is ministry that presents the true Word of God, without fear or favor, and a minister who serves for the glory of God, not the rewards of the church. We need to be alert to the danger of the church imagining that it employs rather than God calls, and of the minister pleasing men rather than God. We need to ask whether we are really open for God to work among us as he wants to" (Jackman, *Judges, Ruth*, p. 267).

Questions 7-8. "Judges 18:1 states that the tribe of Dan 'was seeking an inheritance for themselves to live in, for until that day an inheritance had not been allotted to them as a possession among the tribes of Israel.' We are not to understand from that statement that Dan had been omitted when Joshua divided up the land. Joshua 19 makes it clear that their assigned portion was between Ephraim and Judah, stretching out to the Mediterranean. Dan had refused to trust God by driving out the Amorites. As a result, Judges 1:34 indicates that Dan was forced into the hills and reduced to living in two towns. Dan was left with two choices. As a tribe, they could repent of their unbelief and trust God to keep his word as they entered into battle against their enemies. That was God's will. Or they could look for a new area, a comfortable place where the natives were unprepared, undefended and vulnerable to a sneak attack. Dan chose the easy place and the easy way. They found it far to the north in Laish, a quiet area colonized by some Phoenicians, who were isolated from any allies. God had called Israel to war, and Dan had refused to fight His battle. But it was not because they were committed to peace. They were dedicated to ease. Why fight Philistines when you can blitz Laish? Why stand when you can run? Dan's love of ease went hand in hand with their turning to idols. The five spies did not go to Shiloh to discover the will of God. They went to Micah's shrine and hired a priest. They knew what the living God wanted, but they wanted a man-made god who would fit their life-style without making any demands. That is why, before they ever attacked Laish, they seized Micah's idols and set up Jonathan to be their priest" (Inrig, *Hearts of Iron, Feet of Clay,* pp. 277-78).

Question 9. Revelation 7:5-8 speaks of the 144,000 from the twelve tribes of Israel who have been sealed by God. The tribe of Dan is conspicuously missing from that list.

Question 10. The author of Judges tells us that the problem in Israel was a lack of authority. In this leadership vacuum, everyone was doing as they wished. The church has many authorities to help keep us theologically sound. Most important, we answer to the authority of the Bible and the Holy Spirit. You might also mention the authority of Christ's and the apostles' teaching (which we have in the Bible). Today's churches have pastoral leadership, but the pastors must answer to the authority of the bodies that ordained them. You might talk about your church's authority structure, how it works and how an errant member or teacher is disciplined.

Study 12. Judges 19—21. Why Morality Matters.

Purpose: To illustrate what happens to a society that ignores God's commands for morality.

General note. Because of the length of this Scripture passage, you may want to ask your group to read it before coming to the group meeting. You can ask each of your group members to be prepared to summarize the events of one of the chapters.

Question 2. The Levite sacrificed his concubine in order to save his own skin, uphold the rules of hospitality, and keep the men of Gibeah from committing homosexual rape. The entire tribe of Benjamin was sacrificed in order to punish one city. The whole city of Jabesh Gilead and all its inhabitants were sacrificed in order to keep a tribe from becoming extinct. The young maidens of Shiloh were sacrificed so that the men of Israel wouldn't have to break a vow.

Question 3. "It is not only the action of the men of Gibeah which reveals the abysmally low moral standards of the age; the indifference of the Levite, who prepared to depart in the morning without any apparent concern to ascertain the fate of his concubine, and his curt, unfeeling command when he saw her lying on the threshold (19:27-28), these show that, in spite of his religion, he was devoid of the finer emotions. The sense of outrage does not appear to have influenced him until he realized that she was dead, when he lifted her body on to one of his asses and continued the journey. The whole shocking incident made an indelible impression upon Israel, and was referred to by the prophet Hosea as one of the greatest examples of corruption (Hosea 9:9, 10:9)" (Cundall, *Judges and Ruth,* p. 198).

Question 5. "The public demonstration of sympathy for the Levite was an impressive one. . . . But one could scarcely call it a reasoned response. After all, the appeal had been a thoroughly emotive one. Though the Levite may have lacked the facilities that modern media could have given him, he had three things which produced the desired result: a corpse, a knife, and an unerring instinct for what the public relishes. . . . Just as we need to remind ourselves not to feel too sorry for the wronged Micah in chapter 18, we have to admit that here likewise the wronged Levite is steadily forfeiting our sympathy. He has heavily edited the version of the affair at Gibeah which he presents to the assembly at Mizpah. No one would suspect from it that any folly or callousness of his own might have contributed to the death of the girl. Inflamed by the startling publicity and misled by the selective evidence, the assembly instantly resolved on a quite disproportionate punishment for Gibeah" (Wilcock, *Message of Judges,* p. 170).

Question 7. "They demand an answer from God as to why he has allowed their own actions to produce such devastating results; but there is no reference to any acceptance of blame or confession of sin, unless verse 4 is meant to signify this. It seems more likely that the offerings speak of a glib assumption that their relations with God are intact, and that if they do what is ritually required, he will get them out of their predicament. How often we think the same way! And how we need to learn, as much as they did, that 'to obey is better than sacrifice, and to heed than the fat of rams' (1 Sam 15:22). Significantly, there is no answer from God at all. His judgment has fallen; but the absence of any true repentance ensures the absence of any divine guidance.

He has given his people up to the consequences of their sin" (Jackman, *Judges, Ruth,* p. 302).

Question 8. Jackman points out that the leaders could have simply acknowledged that their oath was foolish and repented: "But their hearts were too spiritually hardened to think of that. Instead they look for a way of keeping the oath, by using a scapegoat. Jabesh Gilead had refused to come up to Mizpah at the time of the national council and was therefore deemed guilty, by association with Gibeah (vv. 8, 9). Another episode of senseless violence follows (vv. 10-12) in which the whole city is exterminated apart from four hundred young virgins who are to become the wives of the six hundred Benjamite survivors at Rimmon. It seems almost incredible that they could try to remedy the effects of one massacre of their own people by another, but that is where sin always leads" (*Judges, Ruth,* p. 303).

Question 10. Our reaction toward sin is usually either to condemn it fiercely or else to condone it. The Israelites seem to have tried first one approach and then the other. God, however, always punishes sin, and yet he forgives it through his own sacrifice. He is the judge who administers both justice and mercy simultaneously.

Question 11. " 'Every man did what was right in his own eyes' means that the people themselves, individually and corporately, had the responsibility of checking ungodliness and promoting holiness. The question was, where did Everyman's 'own eyes' look to find the authority which would tell him how? In practice he regularly looked into his own sinful heart. But in theory there was no reason why he should not have looked somewhere much more trustworthy. . . . The revealed will of God in the words he has given is there all the time, and may be read plainly by the clear-sighted and obedient. 'If your eye is sound, your whole body will be full of light,' and doing what is right in your own eyes will take on a new meaning . . . instead of the moral chaos of chapters 19—21, every circumstance of daily life acknowledging the Lord's authority and reign" (Wilcock, *Message of Judges,* pp. 174-75).

Question 12. "The lesson, then and now, is that a society that refuses to accept guilt, in the sense of distinguishing right from wrong and punishing the offender, will soon prove impossible to govern. Everyone will do what is right in his or her own eyes, and there will be no ultimate restraints. Might becomes right, and civilization ceases. The principle is clear and can be seen to have application to self-discipline, to family life, to a community, state or nation, as well as internationally. It is also relevant to the church of Jesus Christ, whether locally or universally. The tragedy of Israel was that these symptoms were not dealt with when they first appeared, because there was no king. Those of us who are entrusted with authority within the biblical structures of home, church, or nation, have a heavy responsibility before God to use it responsibly in love to him and to our neighbor" (Jackman, *Judges, Ruth,* p. 294).

Donald Baker is the pastor of Reformed churches in Doon and Lester, Iowa. He is also the author of the LifeGuide® Bible Studies Decisions: Seeking God's Guidance; Joshua: The Power of God's Promises; Philippians: Jesus Our Joy *and* Thessalonians: How Can I Be Sure?

What Should We Study Next?

A good place to continue your study of Scripture would be with a book study. Many groups begin with a Gospel such as *Mark* (20 studies by Jim Hoover) or *John* (26 studies by Douglas Connelly). These guides are divided into two parts so that if twenty or twenty-six weeks seems like too much to do at once, the group can feel free to do half and take a break with another topic. Later you might want to come back to it. You might prefer to try a shorter letter. *Philippians* (9 studies by Donald Baker), *Ephesians* (11 studies by Andrew T. and Phyllis J. Le Peau) and *1 & 2 Timothy and Titus* (11 studies by Pete Sommer) are good options. If you want to vary your reading with an Old Testament book, consider *Ecclesiastes* (12 studies by Bill and Teresa Syrios) for a challenging and exciting study.

There are a number of interesting topical LifeGuide studies as well. Here are some options for filling three or four quarters of a year:

Basic Discipleship
Christian Beliefs, 12 studies by Stephen D. Eyre
Christian Character, 12 studies by Andrea Sterk & Peter Scazzero
Christian Disciplines, 12 studies by Andrea Sterk & Peter Scazzero
Evangelism, 12 studies by Rebecca Pippert & Ruth Siemens

Building Community
Christian Community, 10 studies by Rob Suggs
Fruit of the Spirit, 9 studies by Hazel Offner
Spiritual Gifts, 12 studies by Charles & Anne Hummel

Character Studies
David, 12 studies by Jack Kuhatschek
New Testament Characters, 12 studies by Carolyn Nystrom
Old Testament Characters, 12 studies by Peter Scazzero
Women of the Old Testament, 12 studies by Gladys Hunt

The Trinity
Meeting God, 12 studies by J. I. Packer
Meeting Jesus, 13 studies by Leighton Ford
Meeting the Spirit, 10 studies by Douglas Connelly